MYSTIC
MICHIGAN
Part Four
IV

By Mark Jager

Second Edition

MYSTIC MICHIGAN
PART FOUR

By Mark Jager

Published by
ZOSMA PUBLICATIONS
PO Box 24
Hersey, Michigan 49639
zosmabooks@gmail.com

Copyright 2005 by Mark A. Jager
Second Edition Revised Volume Four 2011

Cover Photo Indian Trail Tree
By Deana Jager
Copyright 2009

ISBN 0-9672464-9-0

Dedicated to the memory of my father;
Les Jager, who always encouraged me, supported me,
Loved me and showed an interesting what I was
doing. I will always love him and
he is greatly missed.

Contents

Indian Trail Trees

Just as GPS, maps, and highway markers lead us through the varied paths of highways and road systems across Michigan today, there are ancient signposts that are still in existence that once led people to important destinations long ago. Hidden in the forests and off the beaten paths are venerable figurations that lead to significant historical places known as "Indian Trail Trees" and they can be discovered throughout Michigan if you know what to look for.

Historically, Indians would mark trails, camps, springs, food and even buried treasure by bending a tree to point in the direction of the objective.
They would take a young sapling and bend it at a right angle; pointing in the direction of the path, then secure it by tying a piece of rawhide, a strip of bark, or a vine to a rock. The tree from then on would grow in a perched "L" shape, pointing (even to this day) to the desired route. The point of the bend upward is usually marked by a prominent bump that resulted from cutting the bark and packing it with moss or charred bark. Sometimes the Indians would mark the tree with their initials or tribal symbol.

They would periodically bend the trees along the path so they could easily identify a long course. If the trail crossed a large field or open area they would use rock piles, poles or other materials as markers.

These living guideposts have been estimated to be from 100 to 300 or more years old and many have been found in the Mississippi Valley and the eastern half of the United States. The majority are found in Michigan, Kentucky, Indiana, Illinois, Ohio, Wisconsin and Missouri.

A watchful eye on the lookout may discover one of these historical treasures while walking in the forests of Michigan. Our gratitude to Mr. Bion Jacobs for showing us the beautiful Indian Trail Tree located north of Hersey, Michigan and featured on the cover of this book.

For the sake of future generations, please promote the preservation of these historical trees!

Ruins of Michigan's Lost City

Through the forest, you can see what appear to be the ruins of an ancient city. How can this be? You are in a woodland area near Baldwin. Going on, you see what looks like ancient Roman archways and aqueducts. Some of the arches are 30 feet tall. You see walls that may be three feet thick and are over 20 feet tall.

Also, coming into view are enormous caverns. The caverns look as if they were once lined with bricks. There are also very large basement areas. The outline of at least one of them is the size of a good part of a football field. They are all that remain of titanic buildings that once stood in this location. Trees are coming up through the former floors of the basements that tower 30 feet or so.

In at least one of the former basements is a tunnel filled with water. The end of it can't be observed because of darkness. A second tunnel is not filled with water. After walking through it a number of feet, a person will emerge from a subterranean chamber in a different location. A considerable distance can be traveled underground. There are tall cement towers that take on the look of an obelisk. There are openings in the ground that drop down 20 feet into areas with concrete floors. All throughout the woods cement structures can be partially observed hidden amongst the trees. One begins to wonder how many tunnels, towers, and other structures are obscured out there.

Believe it or not, such a place does actually exist in Michigan. It is located on private property near Baldwin. The ruins are literally what are left of the Michigan ghost town of Marlboro. Marlboro can be located on old Michigan maps. The town had nearly 70 homes at one time. The massive cement structures were built nearly 100 years ago, and placed in various places by the town's cement company. The ruins are on private property now and can't be entered without the permission of the owner. For more information, contact the Baldwin Historic Society.

Michigan's Mystic Tower

A certain Michigan light tower seems to beckon from the great beyond. It twinkles out its ghostly code to mariners on the inland sea of Lake Huron.

The lighthouse at Presque Isle has been shocking observers for several years now. This is because a number of people claim that they have seen the lighthouse doing something that hasn't been scientifically explained. According to a story that appeared in the Bay City Times (Oct 27, 2000), the lighthouse is exhibiting a strange light at the top of its tower. This wouldn't be so unusual if it weren't for the fact that all of the electricity has been disconnected from the tower for decades.

According to The Bay City Times, lighthouse keeper George Parris and a Coast Guard Officer disconnected all of the electrical wires and removed all of the gears, switches and the bulb from the lighthouse in June of 1979. In spite of this, many people have reported seeing a glowing amber light at the top of the lighthouse.

The Bay City Times reported that the odd light appears nightly. Some people think that the mysterious light is simply reflected light from the moon or passing boats. The widow of the old lighthouse keeper publicly announced that she believes that the strange glow is the spirit of her late husband beckoning the townspeople.

Whatever the explanation is for the light, there are many people who have claimed to have seen it. Bay City Times photographer Rick Gillard and reporter Kathie Marchlewski claim to have witnessed this phenomenon first hand while investigating the tower for their newspaper.

Michigan- a Massive Ancient Cemetery

According to reports, in 1890 James O. Scotford of Edmore was hired to erect a fence around a cattle range in Montcalm County for James Remick. While building the fence, the line ran across a small hill about 30 feet across.

While digging a hole for a fence post, the post hole digger struck something hard. Prompted by curiosity, he dug the object up. To his utter amazement he found it to be a large earthen casket.

He took the casket into Edmore and showed it to the townspeople. He also showed it to the citizens of Wyman, a village 3 miles away. Excitement filled the town. Many of the villagers searched the forests and found numerous small mounds and hills.

Before too long, villagers had gone around the area and opened up between 400 to 500 mounds and discovered approximately 100 small boxes. Many other artifacts were found including clay tablets. Some of the relics are reported to have been beautifully carved with ancient Bible scenes, historic scenes, symbols and writing.

A man named M. E. Cornell wrote a book that described the discoveries of the people of Montcalm County. Cornell described the mounds' contents in the following way. "Many curious things were unearthed, such as caskets, tablets, amulets of slate stone, cups, vases, altars, lamps of burnt clay, copper coins hammered out and rudely engraved with hieroglyphics. The cists (small boxes) are of sun dried clay, and are covered with picture writing and hieroglyphics. The cists seem to be intended receptacles for the tablets of record. They have close fitting covers, which are cemented on with Assyrian like cement, and various figures were molded on the top: the ancient sphinx, beasts, serpents, human faces with headdresses or crowns, etc."

In 1907, Daniel E.Soper, who at one time was Michigan's Secretary of State, became interested in Michigan's prehistoric race of people. In G. Major Tabors' book "Prehistoric Man" Tabors wrote the following report of Secretary of State Soper's archaeological find. "By personal effort he (Soper) opened up 117 mounds, some of them within a 10 mile radius of Detroit. In several mounds he found 14 clay pipes, no two alike, and on a stone tablet there is a displayed representation of Adam and Eve, the flood, Noah's Ark with the dove seeking dry land, and animals leaving the ark, besides the temple of sun worshippers."

According to reports, on March 1, 1916 an article appeared in the Chattanooga News in Tennessee after Soper had moved to Tennessee. The article stated that Soper had been in Michigan for nine years. He had dug in various mounds of the ancient mound builders. He had collected hundreds of remarkable relics of the mysterious race which once inhabited Michigan and the Great Lakes basin of North America.

According to literature, on September 18, 1916 the Washington Post reported "Prehistoric tablets of great value found by Dr. Hyvernat in Michigan." The article stated that, "On September 12, Dr. Henri Hyvernat of the Catholic University of Washington D.C. took from a mound in the woods north of Detroit a slate tablet about a foot long with a circular calendar engraved on one side."

Another man from Detroit, James Savage, also excavated relics. Savage was quoted as saying, "We are confident that we are only on the borderland of a great prehistoric people."

In 1817, Mr. Brickenridge, a historian of Jackson County wrote, "The great number and extremely large size of some of them (ancient cities) may be regarded as furnishing, with other circumstances, evidences of antiquity. I have sometimes been induced to think that at the period when they were constructed, there was population here (in Michigan) as big as that which once animated the borders of the Nile or Euphrates or of Mexico. I am perfectly satisfied that cities similar to those of ancient Mexico of several thousand souls have existed in this country." (History of Jackson County, Brickenridge, Page 20)

Do the caskets and burial mounds of Michigan have something to do with this ancient civilization? According to literature, on August 26, 1911 an article appeared in a Detroit newspaper. The article stated that it was believed that a large portion of the entire state of Michigan was a great ancient burial ground. It is reported that by 1911 so many mounds had been opened in Michigan that it appeared as if a large potion of the state was nothing more than a titanic ancient cemetery. Mr. John Russell, one of the researchers, stated that he believed that the old cemetery stretched all the way from Jackson County through Washtenaw County and into Wayne. Thousands of mounds were opened and explored. Some pilgrims knew that these mounds didn't look like Indian mounds. They wondered whose descendants they were, Shem, Ham, or Japheth's. As late as 1977 groups were still coming to Michigan to look for the relics of the ancient civilization. (See Escanaba Daily Press, Tuesday, Dec. 27, 1977)

Although many of these artifacts can still be seen around the country, there is still controversy surrounding there authenticity. The Detroit News published articles in the early 1900s claiming that counterfeiters forged many of the relics. There were also many archaeologists who claimed that nearly all of the relics were just a deception. They claimed that all of the 22,000 tablets were planted by pranksters throughout the state. It is rumored that the relics have never even been carbon dated. The mounds of Michigan are a reality and the objects taken out of them really do exist. Whether a person believes the artifacts were placed there by an ancient civilization or by pranksters all depends on which "experts" one chooses to believe.

Michigan 1999 Fireball Phenomenon

On November 16, 1999, blue-green- orange fireballs began raining down over the skies of Northern Michigan. At 7:11 p.m. the phones began ringing at Wexford County law enforcement agencies. Various people witnessed the rain of fireballs.

According to a front page newspaper article published by the Cadillac Evening News on November 17, 1999, Emily Roncari of Tustin saw an oval shaped light moving in the southern skies. "To me it looked like one big sphere. As it went to the east, it looked like it broke up into five different pieces." Emili Roncari's dad, Ed Roncari saw the object for several seconds. In his opinion, the objects looked like flying machines. "We saw crafts," he said. "There were four of them, all in a line with each other. They moved noiselessly, low, tree top height, but in the distance. Do you know how jet liners have signal lights always blinking? This was a straight line, not blinking. They were tan yellow as I saw them. I've seen shooting stars. They're fast, this was slow." Sheriff's departments in Wexford, Lake, and Grand Traverse Counties received many calls during the event.

Subterranean Worlds

Far beneath our feet is an incredible Michigan underground world. There are a variety of different places all throughout Michigan that contain miles of caverns that remain unknown to most Michiganders.

Did you know that there are vast subterranean areas underneath the city of Grand Rapids? Old gypsum mines have been converted into storage areas. Large semis actually drive down underground roads to subterranean warehouses to pick up goods. There are people who actually work underground. There are nearly 6 miles of underground tunnels in Grand Rapids just at one business alone. The Michigan Natural Storage Company is 80 feet underground. Food, microfilm, and computer records are stored at an underground warehouse.

The underground storage company covers 45,000 square feet. The company at one time conducted group tours. Domtar Corporation operates an underground gypsum business 100 feet beneath Butterworth Avenue, and there is another mine near the Kent County Airport.

The city of Detroit is known for its salt mines. One of the best known is the Detroit Salt Mine. In order to reach the mines you have to descend 1,400 feet. There are over 100 miles of tunnels at the business. The mine spreads out over 1,500 acres. (for pictures see www.detroitsalt.com)

There are also large caverns in the Upper Peninsula. One of the best known is the iron mine at Iron Mountain. At the mine, people can ride a small train into the earth. Underneath the adjoining Michigan cities of Negaunee and Ishpeming there are nearly 180 miles of abandoned mines. There are such vast caverns underneath Negaunee that huge sections of the town have literally caved in.

There are also other smaller underground areas underneath Michigan cities. One such place is underneath Cadillac. There are underground passages in the older section of town which lead to many different downtown businesses. The passageways were used to bring coal to the establishments years ago. There may be such passages beneath many Michigan cities.

The Hemlock Lights

A strange and unusual lighting phenomenon was often seen in the forest regions between Hemlock and Merril, Michigan from the mid 1960s to the early 1980s.

"The lights were fog or something like it," said Viki Buckley of Merill. He fog like formation was illuminated. It would actually float and move around. There were some areas that were brighter than others. The fog emitted a very dull glow. You couldn't explain where it came from. It would grow brighter and dimmer. It never really got that bright."

Buckley mentioned that the hemlock lights were quite popular in the 1960s. At that time there was an old barn out in that area that an old man had committed suicide in. Since the early 1980s many homes have been built in the area. Buckley mentioned that she hasn't heard much about the lights in recent years. However, it is still a possibility that the eerie illuminated fog may be seen in certain areas.

Vicki Buckley's brother in law also commented on the lights. "It did happen in my time era," he said. "Many people figured it was the moon or stars shining on swamp gas." One woman commented on her encounter. "I was sitting down at the end of a dirt trail. The light became greater and brighter. It got so bright that it lit up the whole inside of the dash, and then it vanished," she said. The lights were often seen off M-46 near Steel Road.

Treasure Island Hermit

A mysterious hermit once lived on a small 30 acre island now called Treasure Island off of Point Comfort on the southwest side of Higgens Lake.

For a large number of years before 1900, a man named Israel Porter Pritchard settled on the island. People called him the hermit of Higgens Lake. There are some who say the old man went into hiding following the accidental death of his wife who many believed he had murdered.

The hermit occupied a small cabin for many years and then vanished. His cabin was found vacant when campers investigated it one summer. In 1929, Lloyd L. Harman of Higgens Lake said that several years after the hermit had disappeared he returned to find that his cabin had been burned down. In the summer of either 1902 or 1903 his corpse was found and removed from the island by authorities. Even to this day the hermit is occasionally thought of and mentioned. One may wonder how many odd island dwellers there may be in Michigan.

Strange Animal Encounters

Sometimes Michiganders see things that surprise them and have no logical explanation.

On September 23, 1984, a female motorist reported to Detroit authorities that she had seen a kangaroo hop across I-94 near the Detroit Metropolitan Airport. A kangaroo was also reported by sheriff's deputies the next day. The strange thing is, the creature was never found.

In May of 1984 a large black panther was witnessed lurking in the residential areas of Manchester, Michigan. In August of the same year there were five sightings of a black panther near the Fisher Body Plant in Flint, Michigan.

According to a book called Curious Encounters, a strange encounter took place in Saginaw in 1937. A resident reported that he had seen a man like water creature climb up a river bank, lean against a tree, and then jump back into the water. The person who had seen the creature is reported to have had a nervous breakdown. In addition to this, the D.N.R. gets 10 to 12 calls each year from people who think they have seen Michigan mountain lions. Mountain lions were historically found in Michigan.

Lake Erie's Fairy Grotto

An incredible island with amazing caves filled with
brilliant sparkling gemstones lies in the mysterious waters of Lake
Erie southeast of Detroit.

South Bass Island is the home of 20 spectacular caves.
Two of the caves, Crystal Cave and Perry's Cave contain
fascinating features and are open for public viewing. Crystal Cave
has celestite in it. Celestite is a white mineral containing
strontium. In the cavern, water mineralized with celestite,creating
gem like formations. Some of the crystals from the cave are now
on display at the Smithsonian Institute in Washington D.C. The
cave is beautiful and has earned the name of "The Fairy Grotto."
A cave guide once claimed that many people have come to the
cave in order to place coins in the caves wishing well.

The other main cave, Perry's Cave, also has interesting
features. The two caves have been open for public viewing since
the late 1800s. In the past, colored lights were placed in the cave
to highlight the gemstone features.

The island is captivating and at one time was the home of a
tremendous palace/hotel with over 600 rooms. Even in the modern
day there are some dazzling structures on the island. There are a

couple of interesting stone pillared Greek styled buildings on the island, and in between them stands the third tallest national monument in the United States, Perry's International Peace and Victory Monument. The monument commemorates the American victory over the British during the battle of Lake Erie.

The monument is made out of 80,000 feet of pink granite. It was built from 1912 to 1915 and towers 352 feet above the island. The monument is capped with an 11 ton bronze urn. In addition to these interesting features, there are also vineyards on the island, as well as three museums. Perry's Cave can be contacted at 419-285-2405, Crystal Cave at 419-285-2811. The island is actually in Ohio, but is close to the Michigan border.

Michigan's Underwater Forest

Researchers from the University of Colorado's Institute for Research in Environmental Sciences have claimed to discover that Lake Erie was subjected to a cataclysmic flood several thousand years ago which caused the lake to spill out of its borders. The flood is reported to have swallowed up enormous forest lands near Detroit, southeast Michigan, and Ontario Canada, creating a huge underwater forest. The flood also buried human settlements and is believed by some researchers to be responsible for causing the modern version of Niagara Falls.

The Colorado University research team, headed by Troy Holcomb, studied several hundred soundings of the lake to determine the geography of the lake's bottom. The soundings were taken by such organizations as the U.S. Army Corps of Engineers, The Canadian Hydrographic Service, and the U.S. National Oceanic and Atmospheric Administration.

Researchers studying the sounding of the lake bottom discovered a large number of sandbars, ridges, and river deltas on the lake bottom. Researchers believe that several thousand years ago, Lake Erie's water/shoreline levels were between 33 and 50 feet lower than the shoreline water levels are at the present time.

Researcher Troy Holcomb said, "All around the lake you have these features that look like the shoreline features that are in the range of 33 and 50 feet deep." Holcomb believes that before the catastrophic flood the western basin of Lake Erie was dry land. He believes that it was possible to walk from places in southern Ontario, such as Point Pelee, to the south-eastern corner of Michigan and northern Ohio. He also believes that Lake Erie was an inland sea whose level was maintained by rivers flowing into it, along with precipitation and evaporation. He stated that at one time there was not a channel flowing into Lake Erie from Lake Huron. He suggests that water drained from the three upper Great Lakes into outlets near North Bay and down the Ottawa River.

Holcomb believes the Ottawa River outlets became blocked. When this happened, the water levels in the upper lakes began to rise like a bath tub with the taps turned on, until the water levels raised high enough to spill out into Lake Erie. Holcomb believes that one of the consequences of the flood was that Erie began draining out of the Niagara River which caused the recreation of Niagara Falls. It is believed that before this time, Niagara Falls had fallen silent during a several thousand year period of low water levels. The rise in water levels is thought to have left a gigantic underwater forest, and is also believed to have submerged any ancient settlements or civilizations that may have existed at that time.

Michigan Circle and Square

When explorers first came to a place which would later become known as the city of Tecumseh, Michigan, they found a very strange formation.

Near the bank of the river Raisen, at a place once known as Brownsville, was a structure made of earth. Accurate descriptions of this construction have been left by pioneers of the region.

The earthen structure was in the form of a circle joined by a passageway to a square. According to Hinsdale's Archaeological Atlas of Michigan, over 200 years ago there were still remains of cedar posts standing out of the earthen formation which seemed to indicate that at one time the embankments were palisaded. It is reported that in the center of the circle there were a number of pits. Not far from the circle and the square were two other circular enclosures. The purpose of the structure is unknown. There are various theories concerning the circle and the square as well as similar earth designs that have been found in Michigan.

The lights of Denton Road

Many people have reported that there is a strange light phenomenon that occurs in Canton Township, Michigan. A strange ball of light is said to be seen near a bridge that goes over the lower Rouge River, on Denton Road.

One former Canton resident said, "We were driving down Denton Road and we saw a light that appeared to follow our car down the road. I believe the light exists. There are other people I know who claim that the light actually came down and burnt their car."

Over the years, legends have surfaced and the local people have named the mysterious light "the blue lady". Virginia Bailey Parker wrote about the light in a book called Ghost Stories and Other Tales From Canton (The Canton Historic Society).

In October 1999, the Detroit Free Press reported that Sharon Le Dillenbeck' of Canton, had an unusual experience with some of her friends in 1997. Dillenbeck's daughter said the car started going faster at the bridge for no apparent reason. The Ypsilanti Press also did many articles on the strange light. This odd phenomenon has not been scientifically verified, but if you are an eyewitness of this natural oddity we would like to hear your story.

Reappearing Historic Ship

The hull of a 119 year old ship named "The Minnehana" can still be seen from time to time just off the shore of Arcadia, Michigan.

In November of 1999 the waters of the Great Lakes were dropping due to a lack of rain. Arcadia residents who made their way down to the beach were surprised to see that the hull of the 200 foot sunken schooner had appeared along the shore.

It was not the first time the hull of the ship has been seen. The last time the ship's hull was seen was the 1930s when water levels dropped. The four masted Minnehana sunk in the fall of 1893 while carrying 58,000 bushels of corn on its way from Chicago to Point Edward, Ontario.

As water levels rise, the Minnehana disappears. When the water levels go back down it appears again. Years pass between appearances, sometimes decades. However, when the time is right the Minnehana reappears to relay to the living its timeless message of the perils of the inland seas. For more information see the November 29, 1999 front page article possibly available on microfilm from the Traverse City Record Eagle.

Forest Cemeteries

There are a number of cemeteries that are located in highly unusual places in Michigan. One such cemetery is the old Walton Junction cemetery.

The Walton Junction cemetery is a graveyard that contains the dead of a once thriving lumber town. Most of the people now in the cemetery were born in the 1800s. After the lumbermen left the town, its buildings fell into ruins and disappeared. Now all that remains is the cemetery.

The cemetery is found in an unsuspecting place, right out in the middle of the woods. After traveling down a two-track one can find the forgotten cemetery by following a small footpath. The old graveyard is surrounded by rocks that mark its perimeter. There are remains of cemeteries in even stranger places in Michigan.

The cemetery in Cadillac was actually moved across town at one time. The old cemetery was located on Evart Street near Mercy Hospital. For many years after the caskets were dug up and moved across town to the Maple Hill cemetery, people digging foundations for homes on Evart Street were still finding bones.

Michigan's Lost Gold Mine

There was a gold rush in Michigan in the late 1800s. There were several well known gold mines in the Upper Peninsula. Ropes mine was open as late as 1989. However, there was a gold mine open in the Lower Peninsula too. The strange thing about this Lower Peninsula gold mine is that it has vanished in the mists of time, and has become Michigan's lost gold mine.

In November of 1912, gold was discovered on the Flemming farm near Harrisville, in Haynes Township, Alcona County. In 1913, a mine shaft was sunk to a depth of nearly 100 feet. Nearly a year after this, there was an explosion in the mine. The four Dome brothers who did the mining were killed. The mine shaft proceeded to be filled with water. As of 1971, the site of the mine had never been located. This was the last report heard about the mine.

Frank Jozwiak of Harrison at one time owned the property the mine was located on. Jozwiak says his dad told him a story of an old man who lived in a shack near the mine. The old man snuck down to the river's edge while everyone else was involved in sinking a mine shaft. He worked during the summer hauling dirt to his property. He spent all winter panning for gold. Jozwiak said the old man made his living off of the gold for years.

Underwater Metropolis

According to at least two different publications, mysterious stone structures built by an ancient civilization have been discovered by divers in the bottom of Lake Erie.

A team of scientists headed by Australian archaeologists Dr. Anthony Berens have found what appears to be an ancient metropolis. They were studying changes in the bottom of Lake Erie and discovered stone structures in the north central regions of Lake Erie in 260 feet of water.

"We've got sonar readings that clearly reveal a carefully laid out urban area, complete with two large temples or public buildings, a central park like area and several wide boulevards," Dr. Berens is quoted as saying.

Divers have discovered artifacts that date back as far as 1,500 B.C. and that Dr. Berens has been working with a team of U.S. specialists in a federally funded survey of the Great Lakes basins. Paved streets, a public stadium, as well as fountains and temples have been found. Underwater photographs reveal deep clefts and rifts in the streets and walls which indicate that the city was struck by a powerful earthquake before it sank. The source of this info is questionable.

Medieval Michigan

Did you know that there are areas in Michigan that resemble the places and times of the Middle Ages?

There are actually huge Renaissance festivals in Michigan. People come to them dressed in Middle Age clothing to attend medieval events. One such festival is in Holly, Michigan. Lowell Godfrey of Newaygo at one time went to the Renaissance festival every year. Godfrey commented on the event. "At the festival they have full contact jousting and axe and star throwing. There is also a live theater. In addition there are over 50 merchants on hand. You can buy everything from Middle Age weapons to clothing to food. The festival serves huge feasts with 12 to 15 courses. There are minstrels providing music, and Viking storytellers providing entertainment."

There are also a large number of castles which can be observed in Michigan. One of the biggest is located near Canadian Lakes, Michigan. The castle is quite large and looks like an authentic Middle Age castle with the exception of satellite dishes sticking off the side of it. The grounds around the castle are pleasant. There is a large patio on the back of the castle where guests can sit and enjoy themselves.

To relax near the castle may actually bring one into a medieval state of mind. At times there are actually plays and banquets held at the castle. The Canadian Lakes castle is not the only one in Michigan. There are a number of castles elsewhere. One of them is Curwood Castle in Owosso. The castle was built from 1922 to 1923 by author James Oliver Curwood. Curwood wrote several of his novels there.

Perhaps the most well known castle in Michigan is Castle Farms Theater in Charlvoix. The castle was built by Albert and Anna Loeb in 1918. The castle is a replica of a French country estate. Another castle is Bennett Castle in Ypsilanti. It was built by Henry Ford's right hand man, Harry Bennett, in 1929. Bennett's castle was built to protect him from enemies he had made while he was head of security at Ford Motor Company. Bennett's castle has lion and tiger dens, secret doors, tunnels and escape routes as well as two huge gun towers.

Michigan Explosion Oddity

An Ohio man visiting Michigan claims to have witnessed a strange explosion phenomenon. Jack Stephens, was fishing alone on Weatherhog Lake in the Upper Peninsula when the event took place.

"One muggy September evening at around 6:00 or 7:00 p.m. I was out fishing by myself. Suddenly I heard crackles going off in the distance," Stephens said. "The crackles started out slowly, comparable in speed and intensity to what you would expect to hear if it started raining lightly, a drop here, a drop there. Except the sound that I was hearing was not the sound of raindrops, but a sound that was similar to a shotgun being fired."

"Some of the sounds were close by, others were far away. I could hear them exploding randomly. Then, similar in progression to a pattern of going from light rain to a heavy downpour, the explosions started increasing in speed and in intensity and were everywhere around me. The explosions built up to a peak and then suddenly stopped. These things were just going off everywhere. This really happened."

"For a while I thought it may have had something to do with the B-52 bombers that often flew over the lake. There weren't any planes nearby and there wasn't anybody else on or near the lake." Jack Stephens would like to know what caused this.

Strange Earth Design

A strange earth design covering 3 acres is reported to have been discovered in the early 1900s in Bruce Township.

According to Bela Hubbard's book, Memorials of a Half Century, a circular enclosure covering nearly 3 acres was found near the Clinton River in section 3 of Bruce Township. The report says that the circular earthen formation measured 450 by 400 feet. In it were 3 different openings or gates. Inside the circular enclosure near each of the openings or gates was a small mound of earth. In the nearby vicinity of the circular enclosure, 19 additional earthen mounds were found.

Hubbard also refers to mounds which were built of piled stone. The stones were piled to a height of 4 feet. The rock mounds are reported to have been discovered within a mile of the circular enclosure. It is said that skeletons were found under some of the rock piles.

Michigan's Strange Rivers

In the Northern Hemisphere, most rivers flow towards the south. However, there seem to be several Michigan Rivers that flow in the opposite direction. The St. Joseph River meanders through South Bend Indiana, and then turns and flows north. It continues to flow north through Niles, Michigan, on its way to St. Joseph. The river runs past the ruins of an old fort that was built in the late 1700s. The National Canoe and Kayak Association recognize the river's oddity. It has held at least two of its national meetings in St. Joseph.

This is not the only river that exhibits this strange behavior in Michigan. One Northern Michigan man claims that he has seen a river in Michigan's Upper Peninsula that looks like it runs uphill, defying the laws of gravity. He claims that it happened on a section of Yellow Dog River near Independence Lake. This has not been verified at this time.

Michigan's Underwater Roads

There are many scenic and beautiful drives that may be enjoyed in Michigan. However, there are several Michigan roads that you won't be traveling on any time soon, unless of course you happen to own a submarine. The reason for this is that some of Michigan's roads are under water.

Such is the case in St. Joseph, Michigan. The city has maps that actually have three roads on them which are submerged under several feet of water. So you and your family will not be doing any sight seeing or going for a Sunday drive in that area any time soon.

Those with scuba gear may be interested in trying to find the roads, although by this time they may be buried in sand. The waters of that region have also buried a park area and an entire performing pavilion. The park area was used in the early 1900s and became submerged in 1948 when water levels rose due to natural water cycles.

Michigan's House of David

In days of old, various groups of seeking people came to Michigan looking for a spiritual utopia. One such group was an assembly who called themselves the "House of David." They came to Michigan hoping to usher in the 1000 year reign of the Messiah on earth.

Most of the members wore long hair and beards and believed that they were a part of the regathering of Israel. Some of them believed that they were the descendants of the Jewish race. They built incredible buildings that resembled castles in Benton Harbor, Michigan. The architecture is classy, and the wealth it must have taken to build such buildings is staggering.

The need to build was so great that the members of the House of David actually bought an entire island with a mill on it to fill their needs. The island was called High Island. Their leader was a man named Benjamin Purnell. Some of the members of his communities called him king. The House of David still has a printing press where books can be purchased. If you are in the Benton Harbor area, the place is interesting to see.

Michigan's Rock Face

Almost everyone has heard of the stone faces on Easter Island. However, it comes as a surprise to many people that there is a face carved in stone along a Lake Superior beach.

According to Marquette historian Fred Rydholm, there is a sculpted face staring out over Lake Superior at the east end of the Au Train Beach. There are several different rumors as to who actually carved the formation. Rydholm states that credit for the sculpted face is disputed. One rumor about the faces origin is that it was carved by one of two different carvers in the 1920s. The other rumor is that it was carved by the Indians.

The rock face is depicted as staring solemnly out to Lake Superior. His lips are sealed, his outlook stern. He seems to be deep in thought, perhaps contemplating the legends of the lake as he looks out over the great inland sea. One can easily imagine that this face is patiently waiting for the arrival of a long lost mariner.

Island Treasures

Legends have persisted that vast treasures of Mormon gold are hidden on Beaver Island.

Rumors have been whispered for years that when a dissident sect of Mormons was expelled from Beaver Island by King James, they took their share of riches and buried them in Fox Lake on Beaver Island. The possibility of other treasures besides the treasures of Fox Lake has also been mentioned. A woman known as Mrs. Williams, author of a book called "A Child of The Sea" wrote, "The place they chose to secrete their stolen goods was a long point at the lower end of Beaver Island, distant about three miles from the harbor. They called this place Rocky Mountain Point."

Those visiting the island that enjoy treasure hunting or metal detecting may wish to pinpoint these two areas while exploring Beaver Island. There are also enjoyable camping, historic, shopping and archaeological areas on the island that may be investigated.

Michigan's
Geometric Formations

There are incredible claims concerning the geometric formations found in Michigan and in other places around the world. If various researchers are correct, there is something more than meets the eye when it comes to these strange earthen structures found throughout the state.

James Marshall of Illinois has researched the formations for years, and has been quoted in several articles in the Chicago Tribune on the subject. Marshall claims that the formations are connected mathematically over vast distances of thousands of miles.

Bonnie Gaunt of Jackson, Michigan, is a mathematician and archaeologist. She claims that the earthen structures in Michigan and other parts of the world may be ancient Hebrew monuments which contain mathematical information in its measurements relating to the second coming of Christ.

Raymond Capt, a Biblical archaeologist who has studied the Great Pyramid and other archaeological structures throughout the world, also believes that the structures may have been built by some of the descendants of the sons of Noah who he says, migrated here after the flood.

There are a number of other researchers who believe that the structures were built by either the Adeena or Hopewell Indians. There are many different opinions concerning the origin of these age-old monuments found in Michigan. What do you think?

Ancient Underwater structure

Hundreds of feet out in Lake Huron lies what may be an ancient but not forgotten ruin. Gary Nelkie of East Tawas thinks that there may be a man-made structure near Alpena in the waters of Thunder Bay. The giant rock formation is about 2 miles from shore on a huge shoal in about 2 feet of water. Nelkie believes the structure may have been an ancient fish trap built by Native Americans. He bases this idea on an experience he and another person had while they were out kayaking on Thunder Bay.

"While kayaking, we noticed a large school of fish was following us. We paddled into the mouth of the rock formation. The fish followed us into the rock cove and became trapped inside. It seems to me that this is what the structure was made for." Native Americans had many brilliant ways of gathering food.

There may be other structures like the rock formation in Alpena in various areas of the Great Lakes. The area that this structure is located in is near two islands which are natural wild life refuge areas. It is against the law to trespass on them.

Meteorite Impacts

There are actually several islands in Lake Superior that were formed by an asteroid. According to the book Mysterious Islands by Andre Gooch, scientists have reported that a 19 mile wide meteorite hit the Slate Island area thousands of years ago. The cluster of islands is reported to be what is left of the central cone from the original impact crater. On the island there are dramatic cliffs and interesting rock formations which contain unique coloring and patterns. The Slate Islands in Lake Superior have been investigated by scientists on at least two separate occasions.

There have been many meteorite impacts in Michigan. One of the most recent that has come to attention was the impact near Cadillac in 1999. The crash was reported by the Cadillac Evening News. Tim DeZeeuw of Mcbain claims to have heard explosions when the meteorite crashed. "I heard an explosion off in the distance at about the same time frame that the news reported that the meteorite had crashed," he said. DeZeeuw also reported that he had heard dishes rattling in the cupboard and windows vibrating in there frames when the strike took place.

If you have an unusual
fact or phenomenon
about the great state of Michigan
or about an odd Michigander
and would like to see your story
in a future edition of
"*MYSTIC MICHIGAN*",
please send your information to:

Mark Jager
P.O. Box 24
Hersey, Michigan 49639

Explore the Phenomenal in Michigan's Nature –
Discover the Bizarre in Michigan's Past with the
MYSTIC MICHIGAN SERIES

MYSTIC MICHIGAN PART 1-
Pictured Rocks – Floating Island –Largest Living Creature – Sanilac Petroglyphs – The Cadillac to Traverse City Indian Trail – The Legend of Lake Superior – Missaukee Mounds – Underwater Passages – The Ancient Forest – Michigan Pyramids – Michigan's Mystery Culture –Sea Monster – Bigfoot in Michigan – Treasure Troves – Mystery Canal – Michigan Mirage – Sinkholes – Michigan's Place on the Continent of Pangaea – Gravity Hill – Paulding Lights – Waterfalls – Caves – Ancient Volcanoes – Great Lakes Triangle – Strange Prehistoric Creatures – Meteorites – Michigan's Stonehenge – Ancient Michigan Tablets – Dolmen Altars – St. Elmo's Fire – Ghost Fire – Waterspouts – Green Sunsets – Raining Fish – Tornados of Fire – Water Running UP Hill – Ancient Geometrical Gardens – Spirit Island – Strange Shakings in Michigan – Michigan Dust Devils – Michigan Man Eaters – Sinking City – Ancient Statues – Weird Weather Patterns – Vikings in Michigan – The Village of Giants – Bottomless Lakes – The Island of Ill Repute – Ice Storms

MYSTIC MICHGAN PART 2-
Ancient Underwater Indian Trail – Mysterious Ancient Wall – Ancient Rivers of Fire – Michigan's Life Energy Scientist – Kitch-iti-kipi Michigan's Emerald Spring – Vanishing Stream – Mystery Stones – Floating Bridge – Bizarre Bird Attacks – Disappearing and reappearing Lake – Glowing Graves – Dinosaurs in Michigan – Living Headless Animal – Tallest People – Bizarre Deer encounters – Illusions of Gravity – Artesian Will City – Fantastic Ice Caves – Bridge of Stars – Hobos in Michigan – An Unusual Michigander – Above Ground Cemeteries – Ancient Circular Ruins – Invisible Mountain – Fireballs From the Skies – Ball Lightning – Disappearing Land Masses

MYSTIC MICHIGAN PART 3-
Gogamain, Michigan's Kingdom of Darkness – Strange Underwater Fish Sounds – Magical Singing Mouse – Passenger Pigeon – Earthquakes in Michigan – Michigan's Highest Point – Winter Wonderland Snow Secrets – Secret Weather Omens – Subconscious Designs – Strange Glowing Fungus – Cosmic Radio Station – Angel Encounter – Buried City - Faces in the Falls – Incredible Echo Chambers – Tree Tunnels – Invisible Walls – Ghost Towns – The Lake Michigan Blob- Nature Drums – Primitive Rock Paintings- Age Old Disc Factory – Ancient Observations – Mystic Earth Rings – Mysterious Missing Race – Enchanted Forest – Healing Forests – Mazes – Hypnotic Animals – Water Riddles

MYSTIC MICHIGAN PART 4-
Indian Trail Trees - Ruins of Rome – Mystic Tower – Mermaid – Michigan: Ancient Cemetery – 1999 Fireball Phenomenon – Subterranean World – Hemlock Lights – Treasure Island Hermit – Strange Animal Encounters – Lake Erie's Fairy Grotto – Underwater Forest – Michigan's Circle and Square – Lights of Denton Road – Reappearing Historic Ship – Forest Cemeteries – Lost Gold Mine – Underwater Metropolis – Medieval Michigan – Explosion Oddity – Strange Earth Design – Strange Rivers – Underwater Roads – Will-o-wisp – House of David – Rock Face – Island Treasure – Geometric Formations – Ancient Underwater Structure – Meteorite Islands

MYSTIC MICHIGAN PART 5-
Walled Lake – Phantom Train – Oakwood Cemetery Gravity Hill – Phantom Ships – Norway Forest Light – Mystic Stream – The Portage Lake Story – Buried Prehistoric Beast – Bellevue Ruins – Balloon Bombs in Michigan – Haserot Beach Mystery – Unusual Boulder – Huge Ancient Cataclysm – Mysterious Garden Island – Stannard Rock – Strange Grand Rapids Mound – Ancient 1,000 Acre Garden – Disappearing House – Strange Lake Craters – Ancient Stairway – Michigan's Biggest Trees – Mystery Sphere – Labyrinth – Ancient 2 Acre Horseshoe – Underwater Casino – Acid Lake – Shoe Tree – An Amazing Canyon – Michigan's Scandinavian Landscape

MYSTIC MICHIGAN PART 6-
Crop Circles - More Michigan Mastodons - Whispering Waters – Whirlpools - Stationary Whirlwind - Great Lake Sharks - Flying Campfires - Ancient Parking Lots - Iargo Springs - Strange Animal Screams - Underground Factory - Ancient Cemetery Island - Mystic Lights of Paris - Durant's Castle - Meteorite Fires - Hexen Rings - Singing Sands - Michigan's Giant Gem - Underwater Sinkholes - Underwater Mountains - Ancient Buried Forest - Great Lakes Catastrophe - Ancient Underwater Woodland - Natural underwater Monument - Underwater Maze - Michigan's Earthwork Alignments - Michigan Mimetoliths - Ancient River Beds

MYSTIC MICHIGAN PART 7-
Ancient War Mine - The Bottle House - Stone Chambers - Pre- Glacial - Turnip Rock - Eerie Pere Cheney - The Legend of Silver Mountain - Magnetic Abnormality - The Michigan/Wizard of Oz Connection - Ancient Explosion - King Solomon's Mines? - Michigan's Brigadoon - Huge Statues - Echo Canyons - Wilderness Column of Water - Michigan's New Stonehenge - Amazing Dunes - Arrowhead Finds - The Orbs of Nunica Cemetery - Ancient Library of Rock - A Very Large Piece of Copper - Phenomenal Painting - Michigan's Lost Peninsula - Michigan's Continental Divide - The Mystic Rainbow - The River That Flows Both Ways

MYSTIC MICHGANDER
MYSTIC MICHIGAN PART 1 AUDIOBOOK
TRIPPING AMERICA THE FANTASTIC

ORDER FORM
The following items are available by
Mark Jager

Qty.	Item	Total
	Mystic Michigan #1... $7.95	
	Mystic Michigan #2... $7.95	
	Mystic Michigan #3... $7.95	
	Mystic Michigan #4... $7.95	
	Mystic Michigan #5... $7.95	
	Mystic Michigan #6... $7.95	
	Mystic Michigan #7... $7.95	
	Mystic Michigander... $7.95	
	Mystic Michigan #1 Audio Book ... $12.95	
	Tripping America The Fantastic ... $7.95	
	SUBTOTAL	
	SHIPPING	
	SALES TAX 6%	
	TOTAL	

SHIPPING CHARGES
Please send $3.50 for shipping & handling for the first item purchased. Add ¢.25 for each additional item.

THANK YOU!

Name_____

Street_____

City_____State_____Zip_____

Send order with check or money order to:

Mark Jager
PO Box 24
Hersey, MI 49639

Orders ship USPS
Allow 1 week for delivery

Notes

Notes

Notes

Notes